THE RAVEN
Edmund Dulac, 1912

POE
ILLUSTRATED

Art by Doré, Dulac, Rackham and Others

Selected and Edited by Jeff A. Menges

Dover Publications, Inc., Mineola, New York

Bibliographical Note

This Dover edition, first published in 2007, is a new collection of illustrations for the works of Edgar Allan Poe, reprinted from the following sources: *The Works of Edgar Allan Poe*, "Raven Edition" in five volumes, New York: P. F. Collier & Son, 1903; *Tales by Edgar Allan Poe*, New York: Duffield & Company, 1908; *Tales of Mystery and Imagination*, London: George G. Harrap & Co., 1919 and 1923; *The Bells*, Philadelphia: Porter & Coates, 1881; *The Raven*, New York: Harper & Brothers, 1883; *The Bells and Other Poems of Edgar Allan Poe*, London: Hodder & Stoughton, 1912; *The Raven*, Paris: Richard Lesclide, 1875; *Tales of Mystery and Imagination*, Philadelphia: J. B. Lippincott, 1935; *The Poems of Edgar Allan Poe*, London: G. Bell & Sons, 1900; *Selected Tales of Mystery by Edgar Allan Poe*, Philadelphia: J. B. Lippincott, 1909; *The Gold Bug*, Chicago: Rand McNally & Company, 1902; *Tales of Horror and Suspense*, Mineola, New York: Dover Publications, Inc., 2003. (NOTE: Caption punctuation varies according to the original source.)

Library of Congress Cataloging-in-Publication Data

Poe illustrated : art by Doré, Dulac, Rackham and others / selected and edited by Jeff A. Menges.
    p. cm.
  ISBN-13: 978-0-486-45746-8
  ISBN-10: 0-486-45746-X
    1. Poe, Edgar Allan, 1809–1849—Illustrations. I. Menges, Jeff A.

N8215.P63 2007
741.6'4—dc22

                  2007024311

Manufactured in the United States of America
Dover Publications, Inc., 31 East 2nd Street, Mineola, N.Y. 11501

TO NICK

Who appreciates a good dark tale,
and visuals to go along with it

INTRODUCTION

The name "Poe" conjures images that are dark, mysterious, and gothic. His work is full of exaggerated fears and vengeful specters, capable of guiding the reader down a path that would not otherwise be traveled. Full of imaginings that are often little more than suggestions, his tales rely on the reader's perceptions to create tension and uneasiness. It is fertile ground for any illustrator who has the opportunity to work with them. Many of the images that follow were drawn from artists remote in character from the gothic-style horror that Poe has come to epitomize; but all welcomed an opportunity to explore the dark dreams and rich imagination of Edgar Allan Poe.

The moods that Poe's writings evoke, as well as their origins, become clearer when some of the substance of his life is understood. It was no accident that Poe could fabricate nightmares of such magnitude. As an individual, he was beset by paranoia, and it is often the element of fear within his characters that drives many of his tales to the edges of madness. He has left us a body of work that not only changed America's literature, but also had a lasting effect on multiple genres and forms of storytelling worldwide.

Edgar Allan Poe (1809–1849) had a brief and difficult life. He is heralded today— embraced and revered—at many of the sites he once called home. Born into a family of actors in Boston in 1809, Edgar Poe had an unsettled infancy. Before the age of three, his father abandoned the family and his mother died, leaving the young Poe to fall into the care of the Allan family of Richmond, Virginia. He was well provided for in his youth—which included some schooling in England—and he attended the University of Virginia at the age of seventeen. One vice that Poe acquired as a teen was gambling, and his foster father refused to help him with the debt he accumulated while at school; a major rift resulted, and Poe found himself distanced from the only family he had known for most of his life. After the financial failure of *Tamerlane and Other Poems*, his first attempt at publication, he turned to one of the few options available to a young man with few marketable skills—he enlisted in the army.

After two years in the service, Poe went to live with his aunt and a cousin, Virginia Clemm, in Baltimore. Poe would have been twenty at this point, and he had begun work on a second vol-

"I would call aloud upon her name"
LIGEIA
Harry Clarke, 1919

ume of poetry, which was published in 1829: *Al Aaraaf, Tamerlane, and Minor Poems*. Attempts at reconciliation with his foster father were unsuccessful, and Poe eventually lost all the benefit that he might have enjoyed from that relationship. After considering a military career, and attending West Point for a time, he finally abandoned the effort and went on to publish more poetry. Soon, Poe's prose began to appear in newspapers of the day. His writing eventually demonstrated enough skill to land him one of many editorial positions he would hold in the field of publishing, as he resided in various northeastern cities during brief stints at one periodical or another. His editorial work helped hone his skills as a writer, while giving him an opportunity to be published with some degree of regularity. These jobs tended to be relatively short lived, due to Poe's volatile personality and imperious attitude—in at least one instance he was dismissed for drinking (which would prove to be a chronic weakness for him in years to come).

Poe, his aunt, and Virginia, whom he had married in 1835, lived together for brief periods in Richmond, Philadelphia, Baltimore, and New York, while Poe took various jobs at newspapers and magazines. During these years, many of his most famous tales and poems were written, including *The Tell-Tale Heart, The Pit and the Pendulum*, and *The Fall of the House of Usher*. It was the appearance of *The Raven* in 1845 that finally brought Poe celebrity—the public loved the piece, and Poe was treated like a star. Happiness in his marriage, however, was brief, as Virginia was of frail health, and her life was painfully short. In early 1842, she fell seriously ill with tuberculosis; she never fully recovered and died in 1847. Her death left Poe very unstable, and he fell to drinking more regularly—a habit thought to be a contributing factor to his own early demise at the age of forty.

Poe's death is a mystery worthy of his own creation, and remains a matter of controversy to this day. On October 3, 1849 he was found delirious on a Baltimore street, in clothes that were not his own. Although he lingered for four days, he never became coherent enough to explain what led to his dire condition. He is known to have called out for "Reynolds" on the night preceding his death, but little else remains to offer any clues about the events leading up to his premature end.

From IMP OF THE PERVERSE, *Arthur Rackham, 1935*

Poe wrote at a time (the late 1820s to the 1840s) when high-quality illustration could not easily be reproduced affordably or effectively. His earliest efforts were printed without extravagance, but the volumes that were published after his passing became more and more embellished, due to a growing appreciation for Poe's work, as well as new techniques in the printing arts. The industry hadn't yet devised a means of rendering images reasonably faithful to the original until the American Civil War when the demand for illustration warranted the further development of engraving, and advances in machine-based printing meant more publications competing for the public's attention. The earliest illustrations in this collection are French, dating from 1875. Poe had already been gone twenty-five years when one of the leading painters of the Impressionist movement, Édouard Manet, felt moved to record his own vision of Poe's masterwork, *The Raven*. And when color reproduction became available in the first decade of the twentieth century, it wasn't long before Poe's tales became increasingly popular subjects—Becher's plates from 1903 are among the earliest examples of full-color separation. As publishing boomed, so did new visions of Poe's stories. In the annals of the horror genre, perhaps only Bram Stoker and H. P. Lovecraft can begin to approach the level of impact of Poe.

The current volume is a collection of the visual imaginings of illustrators who portrayed Poe's characters and locales. To illustrate is to interpret and depict the written word vis-à-vis imagery, and it is most often produced by someone other than the author. As such, illustration is a collaborative effort, despite the fact that the images are usually created unilaterally by the artist. In sum, the art on the upcoming pages both shines a light on Poe's dark genius as well as embodies the spirit of collaboration at its best.

Jeff A. Menges
April 2007

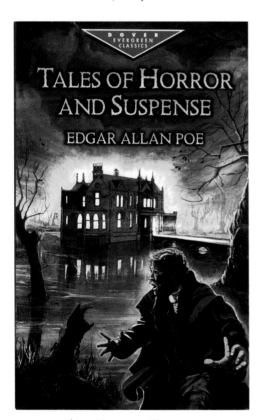

Above: My cover illustration
for the Dover reprint which inspired
the journey that follows.

ARTISTS & VOLUMES

Frontispiece. THE RAVEN. Edmund Dulac, 1912
Title Page. PORTRAIT OF POE, Edmund Dulac, 1912
Tailpiece. UNTITLED, Harry Clarke, 1919

THE PLATES

Opposite: "The beetle . . . glistened like a globe of burnished gold."
THE GOLD BUG
Arthur Becher, 1903

Arthur Becher, 1903

THE WORKS OF EDGAR ALLAN POE

Born in Freiburg, Germany, in 1877, Arthur Ernst Becher (a.k.a. Becker) came to the United States with his family at the age of eight and grew up in the Milwaukee, Wisconsin area. In 1902, he became a student of Howard Pyle's Brandywine School, where he would study until 1904. The artwork for these five Poe illustrations reflects the storytelling and compositional teachings of Pyle, whose influence was discernible in the young Becher. He then went on to became known as a painter of New York and historical scenes, later specializing in depictions of horses. He died in 1960.

"The moment of escape had arrived."
THE PIT AND THE PENDULUM
Arthur Becher, 1903

"I threw open the door and, descending, stood erect in the midst of the party."
NARRATIVE OF A. GORDON PYM
Arthur Becher, 1903

"Upon the whole . . . there was much of the bizarre about everything I saw."
THE SYSTEM OF DOCTOR TARR AND PROFESSOR FETHER
Arthur Becher, 1903

" 'Be that word our sign of parting, bird or fiend!' I shrieked, upstarting."
THE RAVEN
Arthur Becher, 1903

Opposite: THE FALL OF THE HOUSE OF USHER
E. L Blumenschein, 1908

E. L. Blumenschein, 1908

Tales by Edgar Allan Poe

Born in 1874 to modest surroundings in Pittsburgh, Pennsylvania, Ernest Blumenschein received his early instruction from the Cincinnati Art Academy. He followed this career path to studies in Paris, where he met kindred spirit Bert Phillips. Returning to the United States to work in New York as an illustrator in 1896, Blumenschein called that city home until 1919. He is best remembered today for co-founding the Taos Society of Artists, which he formed with Phillips. This group depicted the splendors of the West for a young America that yearned to see it. After many years of summering there, Blumenschein and his wife, fellow illustrator Mary Greene, settled in Taos, New Mexico. They joined their friend Phillips, who had remained since his first trip west with Blumenschein in 1898.

THE MASQUE OF THE RED DEATH

E. L Blumenschein, 1908

THE PIT AND THE PENDULUM
E. L Blumenschein, 1908

THE BLACK CAT
E. L Blumenschein, 1908

THE FACTS IN THE CASE OF M. VALDEMAR
E. L Blumenschein, 1908

THE GOLD-BUG
E. L Blumenschein, 1908

THE MURDERS IN THE RUE MORGUE
E. L Blumenschein, 1908

Opposite: **Tailpiece**
Harry Clarke, 1919

Harry Clarke, 1919 & 1923

TALES OF MYSTERY AND IMAGINATION

The illustrations that Harry Clarke produced for his editions of Poe's work are his best-known efforts today, and remain among the most sought-after images in the archive of Poe's illustrated works. Initially appearing with only his black-and-white pieces in 1919, the book was such a success that the publisher Harrap printed a "deluxe" edition four years later, with an additional eight color plates by Clarke. Although the color work exhibits some of the same design sense that Clarke exhibits in his black-and-white, he was a master inker, and it is those earlier line pieces that represent his legacy today.

Clarke was born in Dublin, Ireland in 1889. As a teen he apprenticed in his father's stained glass studio, learning the nuances of that craft while refining his visual sensibilities. A close examination of Clarke's illustrations will reveal his penchant and strength for working with flat shapes, and understanding the functions of the lines dividing the color or spaces. Throughout his career, Clarke worked in and studied the medium of stained glass, while periodically taking on illustration assignments. Beset by frail health for most of his life, Clarke succumbed to tuberculosis at the age of forty-one.

For the love of God! Montresor! "Yes," I said. "For the love of God!"
THE CASK OF AMONTILLADO
Harry Clarke, 1919

The Earth grew dark, and its figures passed by me, like flitting shadows,
and among them all I beheld only—Morella
MORELLA
Harry Clarke, 1919

But then without those doors there did stand the lofty and enshrouded figure of
the Lady Madeline of Usher
THE FALL OF THE HOUSE OF USHER
Harry Clarke, 1919

The dagger dropped gleaming upon the sable carpet
THE MASQUE OF THE RED DEATH
Harry Clarke, 1919

But, for many minutes, the heart beat on with a muffled sound
THE TELL-TALE HEART
Harry Clarke, 1919

In Death we have both learned the propensity of man to define the indefinable
THE COLLOQUY OF MONOS AND UNA
Harry Clarke, 1923

He shrieked once—once only
THE TELL-TALE HEART
Harry Clarke, 1923

An attachment which seemed to attain new strength
METZENGERSTEIN
Harry Clarke, 1923

And now slowly opened the eyes of the figure which stood before me
LIGEIA
Harry Clarke, 1923

Say, rather, the rending of her coffin
THE FALL OF THE HOUSE OF USHER
Harry Clarke, 1919

Darley, McCutcheon, Fredericks, Perkins, and Riordan, 1881

THE BELLS

In 1881, Philadelphia-based publisher Porter & Coates produced a wonderful gift edition of Poe's *The Bells*. This small gem of a book has twenty-two engravings in total, a portion of which are included here. Porter & Coates, a well-known children's book publisher in the mid-to-late nineteenth century, picked Felix O. Darley to head the list of seven illustrators who were to contribute work to the volume. (Only King and Northam are not included here.) The work was unified under the skills of one engraver, Jas. W. Lauderbach, so that the art maintains the feeling of a single-minded source.

Darley, already a star at this point in his career, was to be the contributor who time would remember best. In fact, according to Walt Reed (author of *The Illustrator in America: 1860–2000*), he "can well be considered America's first important illustrator." Granville Perkins and A. (Alfred) Fredericks would also have lasting careers in illustration, Perkins eventually enjoying success as a marine painter in the New York area.

TO the swinging and the ringing
  Of the bells, bells, bells,
Of the bells, bells, bells, bells,
    Bells, bells, bells,—
To the rhyming and the chiming of the bells.

HOW they scream out their affright!
  Too much horrified to speak,
  They can only shriek, shriek,
    Out of tune,

Opposite:

"From the molten-golden notes" *F. O. C. Darley*
"To the swinging and the ringing" *A. Fredericks*
"Hear the loud alarum-bells" *Granville Perkins*
"How they Scream out their affright!" *R. Riordan*

This Page:

"In the clamourous appealing to the mercy of the fire"
F. O. C. Darley
"Oh, the bells, bells, bells!" *Granville Perkins*
"Hear the tolling of the bells" *F. O. C. Darley*

Opposite: **Eagerly I wished the morrow;—vainly I had sought to borrow**
From my books surcease of sorrow—sorrow for the lost Lenore—
THE RAVEN
Gustave Doré, 1883

Gustave Doré, 1883

The Raven

Paul Gustave Doré was born in the city of Strasbourg, France, in 1832. He became one of Europe's first eminent illustrators. At the age of fifteen he was a regular contributor to the *Journal pour rire,* and was a working book illustrator in Paris by the time he was twenty. The success of some of his early projects caught the attention of English publishers, and in 1853 Doré was asked to illustrate the works of Lord Byron. A steady stream of classical material followed, ensuring him regular work and a long-lasting reputation. In later years, he would turn primarily to religious subjects; Poe's *The Raven* is an exception, and counts among Doré's very last works. It was finished in 1883—the year of his death.

Doubting, dreaming dreams no mortal ever dared to dream before . . .
THE RAVEN
Gustave Doré, 1883

. . . a stately Raven of the saintly days of yore.
Not the least obeisance made he; not a minute stopped or stayed he . . .
THE RAVEN
Gustave Doré, 1883

Till I scarcely muttered "Other friends have flown before—
On the morrow he will leave me, as my hopes have flown before."
THE RAVEN
Gustave Doré, 1883

Then upon the velvet sinking, I betook myself to linking
fancy unto fancy, . . .
THE RAVEN
Gustave Doré, 1883

"... tell me truly, I implore—
Is there—is there balm in Gilead?—tell me—tell me, I implore!"
THE RAVEN
Gustave Doré, 1883

"Be that word our sign of parting, bird or fiend!" I shrieked, upstarting—
THE RAVEN
Gustave Doré, 1883

Opposite: THE CITY IN THE SEA, Headpiece
Edmund Dulac, 1912

Edmund Dulac, 1912

The Bells and Other Poems

By a good measure, the creator of the largest body of work among the volumes considered here, Edmund Dulac (1882–1953) was in his thirtieth year when he made this stellar contribution to the imagery of Poe. As one of England's leading "gift-book" artists in the early years of the twentieth century, Dulac worked on a number of beautiful and well-produced books—classic stories with new color illustrations that were an annual anchor to a publisher's list. Dulac is primarily remembered for his rich and colorful scenes of Eastern tales, as well as a large body of work in a variety of fairy tale collections. The sense of mystery and the exotic nature of Poe's poetry would be fertile material for Dulac's imagination, and he produced remarkable pieces for this Hodder & Stoughton volume in 1912.

The original volume contained twenty-eight full-color plates, and numerous details like those below: line work printed on a neutral tone, to preserve the subtle quality of the original etchings. Among Dulac's pieces are two portraits of Poe—one printed in this collection on the title page, and the other appearing as this book's frontispiece—casting Poe himself as the victim of his Raven. Dulac continued to produce books into the late 1920s, and later turned to other areas of the graphic arts to further his career, working until his passing in 1953.

THE BELLS, Frontispiece
Edmund Dulac, 1912

THE BELLS, PLATE 2
Edmund Dulac, 1912

DREAMLAND
Edmund Dulac, 1912

AL AARAAF
Edmund Dulac, 1912

Top, left to right: ALONE, ISRAFEL
Lower, left to right: BRIDAL BALLAD, THE CITY IN THE SEA
Edmund Dulac, 1912

THE SLEEPER
Edmund Dulac, 1912

Top, left to right: THE BELLS 3, ANNABEL LEE
Lower, left to right: TO THE RIVER, FAIRY-LAND
Edmund Dulac, 1912

ELDORADO
Edmund Dulac, 1912

To Helen

Edmund Dulac, 1912

TO HELEN, PLATE 2
Edmund Dulac, 1912

Édouard Manet, 1875

The Raven

If among the roster of Poe's illustrators there is an anomaly, it is perhaps Édouard Manet (1832–1883). This French Realist painter—whose work depicting contemporary life and landscape inspired the Impressionist movement—embraced the opportunity to work on *The Raven* in 1874. It was one of only three books he illustrated during his career.

Encouraged by a friend and poet, Stéphane Mallarmé, who had prepared a French translation of Poe's *The Raven*, Manet produced a total of eight images for the project, although only six would accompany the final work. The art was done as lithographs, and capture the freshness of brushwork more than any etching or engraving would have. The book was produced in a limited edition of 240 copies, in a large folio format. It was not well received—copies moved slowly—and plans for a second Poe project (*The City in the Sea*) were scrapped. Manet would do only one more book after this one—with wood engravings—in 1876.

Opposite:
Open here I flung the shutter, when,
with many a flirt and a flutter,
In there stepped a stately Raven
of the saintly days of yore

Above left:
TITLE PAGE ILLUSTRATION

Left:
And the Raven, never flitting, still is sitting—
On the pallid bust of Pallas just above
my chamber door

Above:
And my soul from out that shadow that lies
floating on the floor
Shall be lifted—nevermore!

THE RAVEN
Édouard Manet, 1875

Opposite: THE MASQUE OF THE RED DEATH, Tailpiece
Arthur Rackham, 1935

Arthur Rackham, 1935

TALES OF MYSTERY AND IMAGINATION

In the first half of the twentieth century, Arthur Rackham (1867–1939) was arguably the most dominant illustrator of the gift-book market, and remained an active book illustrator during his entire career. Rackham's work on Poe's tales came late in his life, and while much of the work he was doing in the late 1930s had more reserved qualities, Rackham's illustrations for *Tales of Mystery and Imagination* have a great deal of the energy and fluidity of his earlier work.

Worthy of attention are the fantastic black-and-white pieces that appear here. His output of line illustration was considerable throughout his career, and it was not uncommon for a volume that featured his work to contain both color plates and line drawings. Rackham was also quite proficient at silhouette work, an especially popular style of the 1890s. He explored the use of negative space, creating positive images from the white on black, coexisting with images done in the reverse. These skills fortuitously collided here, in a number of the works presented in his Poe collection. The resulting effect is somewhat unsettling—a perfect complement to the dark and otherworldly subject matter at hand.

The eight corpses swung in their chains, a fetid, blackened, hideous and
indistinguishable mass
HOP-FROG
Arthur Rackham, 1935

It grew louder—louder—louder! And still the men chatted pleasantly, and smiled
THE TELL-TALE HEART
Arthur Rackham, 1935

The sentence—the dread sentence of death—was the last distinct
accentuation which reached my ears
THE PIT AND THE PENDULUM
Arthur Rackham, 1935

At length for my seared and writhing body there was no longer an inch of foothold
on the firm floor of the prison
THE PIT AND THE PENDULUM
Arthur Rackham, 1935

I at length found myself within view of the melancholy House of Usher
THE FALL OF THE HOUSE OF USHER
Arthur Rackham, 1935

In their sad and solemn slumbers with the worm
THE PREMATURE BURIAL
Arthur Rackham, 1935

Opposite: ULALUME
W. Heath Robinson, 1900

W. Heath Robinson, 1900

THE POEMS OF EDGAR ALLAN POE

Three brothers—Charles, Thomas, and W. Heath Robinson—may be considered England's first family of illustrators. All three had found marked success in this growing field at the turn of the century. W. Heath Robinson (1872–1944) is probably the most well-known today, due to his memorable cartoons depicting bizarre, complex contraptions for doing simple and mundane tasks. In 1902, he published *The Adventures of Uncle Lubin,* a tale of his own creation where the humor that marked the latter part of his career made its first appearance. While that facet of Robinson's work would give him lasting fame, he had a more serious side, well-suited to book illustration.

The Poems of Edgar Allan Poe was one of W. Heath Robinson's earliest large-scale book projects. It contains over 100 line drawings, from small details to two-page spreads. Along with some beautifully drawn classical figures, his affection for landscape emerges in these pieces, where the settings sometimes dwarf the characters within. They show a superb command of black-and-white line, not too surprising since the Robinson brothers were the third generation in a family consisting of either artists or engravers.

AL AARAAF
W. Heath Robinson, 1900

Above left: TO ONE IN PARADISE
Above right: ALONE
Bottom: LETTER TO MR. ——, Tailpiece
W. Heath Robinson, 1900

Above, left and right: But Evil things, in robes of sorrow, Assailed the monarch's high estate
THE HAUNTED PALACE
Lower: He met a Pilgrim Shadow
ELDORADO
W. Heath Robinson, 1900

Above, left and right: **The Night's Plutonian Shore**
THE RAVEN
W. Heath Robinson, 1900

Above left: **A Valentine**
Above right: **Al Aaraaf**
Lower left: **The Bells**
Lower right: **Where an Eidolon named night on a black throne reigns upright**
Dreamland
W. Heath Robinson, 1900

With its phantom chased for evermore by a crowd that seize it not
THE CONQUEROR WORM
W. Heath Robinson, 1900

Opposite: COVER IMPRINT
Byam Shaw, 1909

Byam Shaw, 1909

SELECTED TALES OF MYSTERY

Although not as well known in the United States, John Byam Liston Shaw (1872–1919), or Byam Shaw as he was known, was a gifted British illustrator who bridged the gap between fine art and illustration. Encouraged to pursue a career in art by none other than John Everett Millais, Shaw embraced Pre-Raphaelite ideals and incorporated them into his work. While many of the other illustrators included in this collection tended toward more fanciful imagery, Shaw preferred classical material, such as *Tales from Boccaccio* and the works of Shakespeare. His work on Poe's *Selected Tales of Mystery* represent some of his most imaginative images, and are indicative of the respect Poe's writing commanded in 1909. In 1910, Shaw and longtime friend and fellow teacher Reginald Rex Vicat Cole opened an art school, which would continue to flourish and bear Shaw's name for more than ninety years.

THE ASSIGNATION
Byam Shaw, 1909

"The thing that was enshrouded advanced boldly and palpably
into the middle of the apartment"
LIGEIA
Byam Shaw, 1909

Above left: "A masquerade in the palazzo of the neopolitan Duke Di Broglio" WILLIAM WILSON
Above right: "Darkness and Decay and the Red Death held illimitable dominion over all"
THE MASQUE OF THE RED DEATH
Lower left: THE CASK OF AMONTILLADO
Lower right: "A Cloud of smoke settled heavily over the battlements in the distinct colossal figure of—a horse"
METZENGERSTEIN

Byam Shaw, 1909

"A magic prison-house of grandeur and of glory"
ELEONORA
Byam Shaw, 1909

Above left: "**Upon the very verge of precipitous descent hovered a gigantic ship**" Ms. Found in a Bottle
Above right: "Yes;—no;—I have been sleeping—and now—now—I am dead"
The Facts in the Case of M. Valdemar
Lower left: The Murders in the Rue Morgue
Lower right: "**I had walled up the monster within the living tomb!**" The Black Cat
Byam Shaw, 1909

"They swarmed upon me in ever-accumulating heaps"
THE PIT AND THE PENDULUM
Byam Shaw, 1909

Opposite:
THE GOLDBUG, Tailpiece
and Frontispiece Map
G. C. Widney, 1902

G. C. Widney, 1902

THE GOLD BUG

Of all of the contributing illustrators, G. C. Widney (1871–?) may have been the least prolific. Although as shown here to be a proficient inker—producing solid line work—Widney was similar to many other illustrators of the period, which may explain why his name does not emerge from the very large group of artists who profited from a time when there was a great demand for their work. Widney, born in Illinois in 1871, studied in Chicago and Paris. In the first quarter of the twentieth century, his name surfaces in book illustration, advertising, and magazines (he was a regular contributor to *The Saturday Evening Post* from 1906 to 1914), but then fades from sight shortly thereafter. His work here is typical of that for magazine fiction of the time, strong and clear, with a nod to the earlier techniques of wood engravers retained in his inking style.

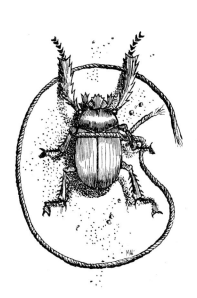

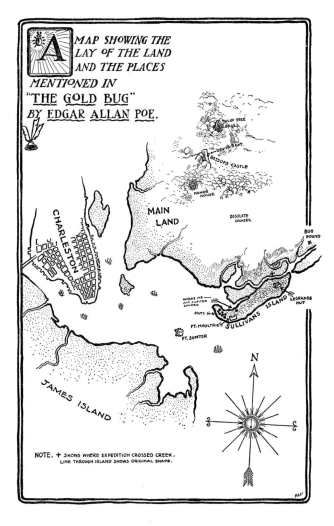

Above left: "This is a strange scarabus, I must confess"
Above right: "With a heavy heart I accompanied
my friend"
Left: "Lor-a-marcy! What is dis here pon de tree?"
G. C. Widney, 1902

Top left: "The lanterns having been lit,
we all fell to work"
Top right: "We found ourselves possessed of even
vaster wealth than we had at first supposed"
Right: "I proceeded to use the glass"
G. C. Widney, 1902

THE
END